The How-to Guide for **KIDS** Meeting **DOGS**
(and **DOGS** Meeting **KIDS**)

May I Pet Your Dog?

by **STEPHANIE CALMENSON**   Illustrated by **JAN ORMEROD**

CLARION BOOKS
New York

To Mark . . . and to Harry
—S.C.

Heartfelt thanks to behaviorist Eve Demian for helping me raise Harry and for sharing her enormous expertise about children and dogs. Thanks, too, to Robin Kovary and Micky Niego for helping me raise my first dog, Rosie, and for leading me to Eve.

Clarion Books
a Houghton Mifflin Company imprint
215 Park Avenue South, New York, NY 10003
Text copyright © 2007 by Stephanie Calmenson
Illustrations copyright © 2007 by Jan Ormerod
Front cover photograph and photograph on page 32 (*bottom*) copyright © 2005 by Ronnie Schultz

The illustrations were executed in watercolor.
The text was set in 16-point Palatino.

www.clarionbooks.com

Printed in Singapore.

Library of Congress Cataloging-in-Publication Data

Calmenson, Stephanie.
May I pet your dog? / by Stephanie Calmenson ; illustrated by Jan Ormerod.
p. cm.
Summary: Harry the dog explains how to safely meet him and his friends.
ISBN-13: 978-0-618-51034-4
ISBN-10: 0-618-51034-6
[1. Dogs—Fiction. 2. Pets—Fiction. 3. Friendship—Fiction. Safety—Fiction.]
I. Ormerod, Jan, ill. II. Title.
PZ7.C136May 2006
[E]—dc22   2005034955

TWP 10 9 8 7 6 5 4 3 2 1

A NOTE TO GROWNUPS

The surest way to keep your child safe around dogs is with your careful supervision. For times when you cannot be present, though, help your child learn as much as possible about dogs. The more your child knows, the safer and happier he or she will be.

WOOF! I'm a dog.
But I'm not just any dog.
I'm a long-haired, chocolate-dappled dachshund.
My name is Harry, and I want to be your friend.

Do you want to be my friend?
Good! I'll tell you how.

When you see me coming, ask my owner,
"May I pet your dog?"
Don't worry. She'll say yes.
I'm a little shy, but I like meeting new people.
And I like kids the best!
Okay, go ahead and ask.

May I pet your dog?

Yes, you may.
Harry loves children!

See? I told you she'd say yes!

Here's what to do next.
Hold your hand out, with your fingers down.
Let me come and sniff it.
That's how I learn about the world.
I use my nose.

Sniff, sniff.

I like to be scratched on my back.
Please come to me from the side.
Don't reach over my head.
That scares me.

I'm soft, right?
You're gentle. That's a good thing.
Always be gentle with dogs.

11

Here comes my friend Twigs.
Do you want to meet her?
Ask her owner, "May I pet your dog?"

Do you remember what to do next?
That's right.
Hold your hand out, with your fingers down.
Let Twigs come and sniff it.

Sniff, sniff.

Oops! Twigs likes you too much!
She's jumping up to lick you.
She's misbehaving!

Her owner will tell her what to do.

Twigs, sit!
Good dog!
You can pet Twigs now.

Twigs is so happy, she's wiggling her whole body! Funny Twigs!

My friend Chester is coming this way.
He's BIG, right? He's nice, too.
But don't take my word for it.
Always ask the owner.

May I pet your dog?

Sure. Chester would like that! He's a gentle giant.

You know what to do.
Hold your hand out, with your fingers down.
Let Chester come and sniff it.
Chester's big, but don't be scared.

Most dogs have a favorite petting spot.
Ask if Chester has one.

Does Chester have a
favorite spot?

He likes to be stroked
on his shoulder.

Look! Chester's thumping his back paw really fast.
That means you found his favorite spot!

It's time for Chester and Twigs to go.
Do you want to say goodbye?

Here comes a dog I don't know.
I'm not sure she's friendly. I'll see if my nose knows.
Sniff, sniff. I don't smell a friend.
You know what to ask.

Did you hear that growl? That means:
Don't come near me.
Don't even look at me.

We'll turn away our eyes.
We'll turn away our heads.
We'll stay perfectly still and quiet
until she passes.

Okay. She's gone. Now it's just us again.
Do you want to see me do a trick?
Ask my owner.

Can Harry do a trick?

Sure. You can help him.
Hold out your hand and say,
"Paw, please."

23

Hooray! My owner has treats.
Would you like to give me one?
Hold your hand out flat with the treat in the center of your palm.
That way I won't nip your fingers by mistake.

Yum! Thank you! I can do other tricks. Do you want to see?
Ask my owner. Tricks for treats!

I hear growling and barking. It's a dog guarding a car.
Some dogs can be unfriendly when they are guarding what's theirs.
Never go near a dog in a car or a truck.

Grrr. Grr-ruff!

I see another dog we shouldn't say hello to now.
That dog is working and can't stop to meet us.
She's guiding someone who cannot see.
Do not interrupt a dog who is working.

Hey! You know what?
You and I are good friends now, aren't we?

That's what can happen when you say,
"May I pet your dog?"

HARRY AND HIS FRIENDS SAY . . .

If you ever see **a dog without an owner,** stay away!

Never put your face
close to any dog's face.

Be considerate. Be safe.
Stay away from a dog who is sleeping, eating, caring for puppies, or chewing a bone, a toy, or a stick.

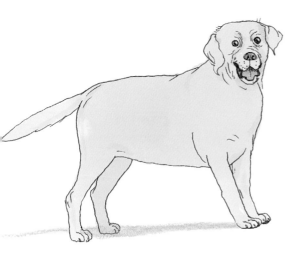

Don't run or shout around dogs.

If you are ever frightened of a dog, turn your head and look away. Then stay perfectly still and quiet. Make believe you are a tree. Or curl up on the ground and be a rock. A dog may sniff a tree or a rock, but he will not hurt or chase one.

Be gentle. Be kind.
Remember, dogs have feelings, too.

31

Harry's Story

I'm the real Harry. When I met Stephanie, I had been living in a cage for three months, waiting for someone to adopt me. I was one sad and scared puppy.

As soon as Stephanie took me home, she saw that I liked children, so she looked for kids who would meet me gently. That's the way all dogs need to be met. Lots of kids were nice to me. Grownups, too. Thanks to them, I'm much braver now. I'm a happy dog with dozens of friends.

Try to learn all you can about dogs. Ask your parents, teachers, or librarian to help you. Look. Listen. Read. And don't forget to ask: MAY I PET YOUR DOG?

One sad puppy

Happy and smiling

E
CAL

Calmenson,
Stephanie.

May I pet your dog?

$9.95